Civil War Is Coming

Christi E. Parker, M.A. Ed.

Table of Contents

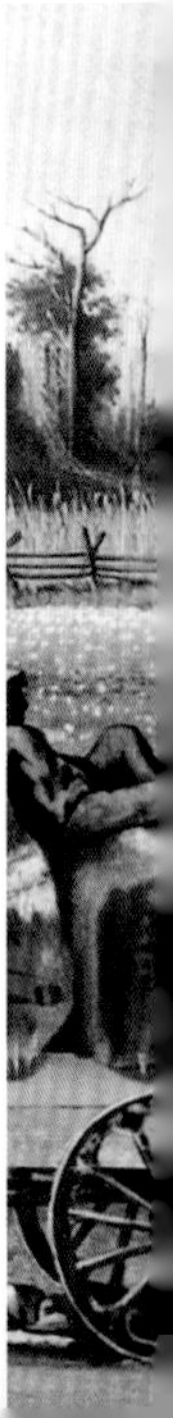

Conflicts Begin

During the 1800s, people in the United States were divided. One of the major issues that divided the nation was slavery. The Southerners did not want their way of life changed. Slaves did much of the physical work on the **plantations** (plan-TAY-shuhnz). Some people in the North did not believe that slaves should continue to be used. This disagreement led to many other problems in the country.

Congress tried to prevent a war by **compromising** (KOM-pruh-myz-ing). But, the compromises were not enough. In 1860, the Southerners were angered by the election of Abraham Lincoln as president. States began to **secede** (suh-SEED) from the Union. A civil war was about to begin.

▼ Plantations were important to the South.

Trying to Compromise

By the 1800s, life in the North and the South was very different. The issue of slavery affected many parts of life. It was important to everyone that there were an equal number of slave states and free states.

New **territories** (TAIR-uh-tor-eez) had formed as people settled the land in the West. Then, after they grew, the territories could become new states. When a new state was added to the Union, new **representatives** were added to Congress.

Who Wrote It?

Henry Clay was said to be the author of the Missouri Compromise. But, Jesse Thomas of Illinois actually wrote most of it. Clay is given the credit because he helped to get the bill passed.

This map shows how the compromise affected the United States.

People in Missouri wanted their territory to become a state. Missouri could either enter the Union as a slave state or a free state. Southerners did not want the Northerners to have more votes in Congress. Northerners did not want slavery to spread further into the West.

In 1820, Henry Clay of Kentucky came up with a plan. Missouri entered the Union as a slave state. The region of Maine separated from Massachusetts. It then became a free state. From then on, all territories above Missouri's southern border were free. All territories below the southern border of the new state were slave. This was called the Missouri Compromise.

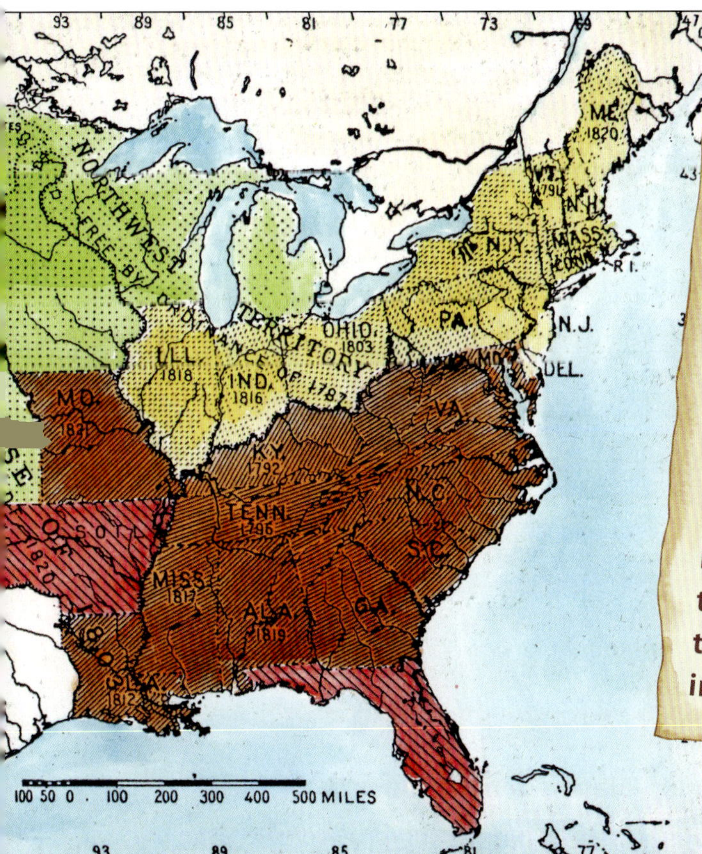

The First Bill

The Missouri Compromise was not the first attempt at a compromise. James Tallmadge of New York wrote a bill that would not allow slavery to grow in Missouri. It also set any children of slaves in Missouri free when they turned 25. This bill passed in the House, but it did not pass in the Senate.

Another Compromise Is Made

In 1850, the free territory of California was ready to join the Union. This would mean that free states would outnumber slave states in Congress. The Southerners were afraid Congress would end slavery. Once again, Henry Clay went to work on a compromise. He helped write the Compromise of 1850.

The Largest Slave Market

At the time the Compromise of 1850 was written, Washington, D.C., had the largest slave market in the United States. More slaves were traded there than anywhere else.

▲ Henry Clay addressing the Senate in 1850

Slave auction house ▶

In this compromise, California entered the Union as a free state. The people who lived in Utah and New Mexico would decide if they wanted to be free or slave. The Fugitive Slave Act was started. And, slave trade was banned in Washington, D.C.

The Fugitive Slave Act stated that all runaway slaves must be returned to their owners. Anyone who helped the slaves could be jailed or fined.

▲ After the Fugitive Slave Act, blacks were in danger of being returned to slavery.

The Underground Railroad

Most of the Compromise of 1850 helped the antislavery cause. However, the Fugitive Slave Act helped slave owners. Years earlier, a route from the South to the North was set up. The route was called the "Underground Railroad." The Underground Railroad was used even more because of the Fugitive Slave Act.

▲ Frederick Douglass (center) and others helped blacks in the United States.

People Against Slavery

Not everyone in the North wanted to end slavery. Many people did not like slavery, but they were not affected by it. They mostly cared about their own lives.

Other people wanted slavery to end quickly, even if it meant going to war. These people were called **abolitionists** (ab-uh-LISH-uhn-istz).

Frederick Douglass was a well-known black abolitionist. He was born as a slave, but he ran away as a teenager. Douglass wrote about his life, gave speeches, and published a newspaper.

William Lloyd Garrison was a white abolitionist. He was jailed many times because he spoke out against slavery. Garrison published a newspaper called The Liberator. He wanted an end to slavery. However, Garrison did not want the country to go to war.

William Lloyd Garrison

Burning the Constitution

Garrison once burned a copy of the Constitution of the United States in public. He believed the document allowed slavery. This was very shocking to people.

▼ This is a copy of Garrison's newspaper from April 1864.

THE LIBERATOR.

VOL. XXXIV. NO. 14. BOSTON, FRIDAY, APRIL 1, 1864. WHOLE NO. 1730.

Refuge of Oppression.

Selections.

The Book That Caused an Uproar

Harriet Beecher was the daughter of a famous preacher. He preached against slavery. Harriet was one of 11 children. Many of the children followed in their father's footsteps. They also spoke out against slavery.

In 1836, Harriet married Calvin Stowe. He was a professor and an author. He wanted his wife to write also. Harriet wrote many books, but she is best known for *Uncle Tom's Cabin*. This is a book about the lives of two slave families. It shows many good and bad parts of slavery.

Lincoln Meets Stowe

Upon meeting Stowe at a White House reception, Abraham Lincoln supposedly said, "So this is the little lady who started this big war!"

Harriet Beecher Stowe

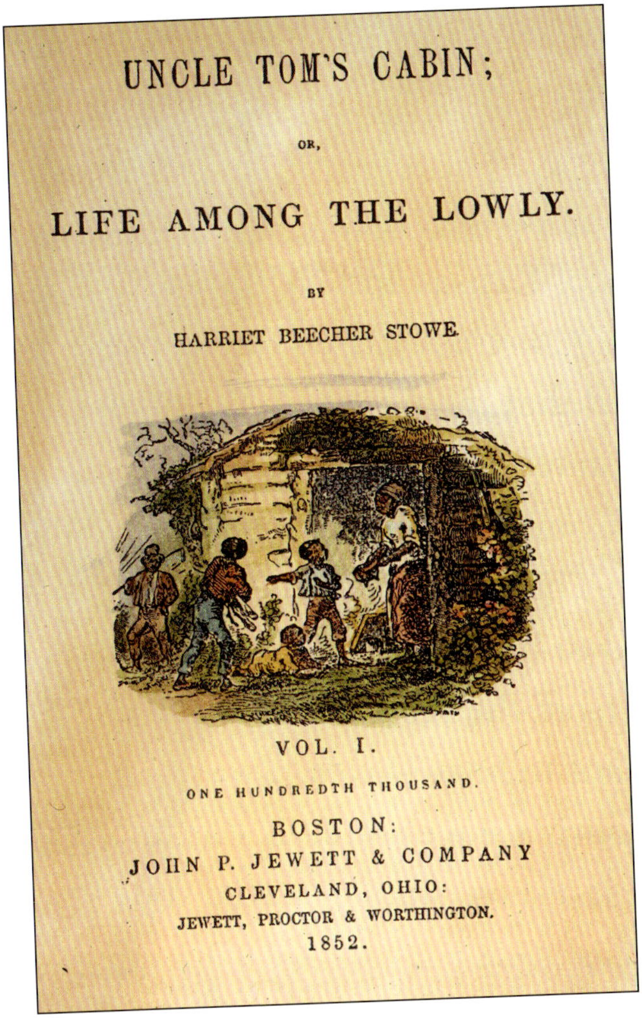

The South's Reaction

Uncle Tom's Cabin made many people in the South angry. Some Southerners were so upset, that if you were caught with the book, you could be sent to jail.

At first, the story was printed for 40 weeks in a newspaper. The chapters were read weekly in homes across the country. The full book was printed in March 1852. *Uncle Tom's Cabin* immediately broke all sales records. It sold 50,000 copies by 1857.

This story helped the antislavery cause. It was more meaningful than protests and preaching. The book had a personal style, interesting characters, and everyday settings. This made the book very popular, especially in the North.

Bleeding Kansas

Once territories had enough people, they could become states. In 1854, the territories of Kansas and Nebraska were ready to join the Union. Congress passed the Kansas-Nebraska Act. This law stated that the people in the areas would vote to decide if their states would be free or slave. This law broke the Missouri Compromise. Both of these states should have been free states. This made many people angry.

People in Nebraska voted to become a free state. Most of the area's population was from the North. So, it was not surprising that they decided not to have slaves.

Kansas was next to Missouri, a slave state. It was unclear whether people would make it a slave state or a free state.

People from Missouri traveled to Kansas to vote illegally.

▲ These men voted on the Kansas ballot.

Tempers Flare

During this time, the men in Congress often argued over slavery. Preston Brooks of South Carolina and Charles Sumner of Massachusetts got into an argument. Brooks was mad after Sumner made a speech against slavery. So, Brooks beat Sumner with a cane. Though Sumner survived, he was no longer able to serve in Congress.

People from the South and the North went to Kansas. Even though they did not live in Kansas, they voted. Based on the voting, Kansas became a slave state.

The Northerners refused to accept the vote. Fights over the vote led to violence. Many small battles were fought and people died. The territory soon became known as "Bleeding Kansas." It was not until 1861 that Kansas finally became a free state.

FRANK LESLIE'S ILLUSTRATED NEWSPAPER

No. 82.—VOL. IV.] NEW YORK, SATURDAY, JUNE 27, 1857. [PRICE 6 CENTS.

(Copyrighted June 22, 1857.)

TO TOURISTS AND TRAVELLERS.

We shall be happy to receive personal narratives, of land or sea, including adventures and incidents, from every person who pleases to correspond with our paper.

We take this opportunity of returning our thanks to our numerous artistic correspondents throughout the country, for the many sketches we are constantly receiving from them of the news of the day. We trust they will spare no pains to furnish us with drawings of events as they may occur. We would also remind them that it is necessary to send all sketches, if possible, by the earliest conveyance.

VISIT TO DRED SCOTT—HIS FAMILY—INCIDENTS OF HIS LIFE—DECISION OF THE SUPREME COURT.

WHILE standing in the Fair grounds at St. Louis, and engaged in conversation with a prominent citizen of that enterprising city, he suddenly asked us if we would not like to be introduced to Dred Scott. Upon expressing a desire to be thus honored, the gentleman called to an old negro who was standing near by, and our wish was gratified. Dred made a rude obeisance to our recognition, and seemed to enjoy the notice we expended upon him. We found him on examination to be a pure-blooded African, perhaps fifty years of age, with a shrewd, intelligent, good-natured face, of rather light frame, being not more than five feet six inches high. After some general remarks we expressed a wish to get his portrait (we had ma le efforts before, through correspondents, and failed), and asked him if he would not go to Fitzgibbon's gallery and have it taken. The gentleman present explained to Dred that it was proper he should have his likeness in the "great illustrated paper of the country," overruled his many objections, which seemed to grow out of a superstitious feeling, and he promised to be at the gallery the next day. This appointment Dred did not keep. Determined not to be foiled, we sought an interview with Mr. Crane, Dred's lawyer, who promptly gave us a letter of introduction, explaining to Dred that it was to his advantage to have his picture taken to be engraved for our paper, and also directions where we could find his domicile. We found the place with difficulty, the streets in Dred's neighborhood being more clearly defined in the plan of the city than on the mother earth; we finally reached a wooden house, however, protected by a balcony that answered the description. Approaching the door, we saw a smart, tidy-looking negress, perhaps thirty years of age, who, with two female assistants, was busy ironing. To our question, "Is this where Dred Scott lives?" we received, rather hesitatingly, the answer, "Yes." Upon our asking if he was home, she said,

"What white man arter dad nigger for?—why don't white man 'tend to his own business, and let dat nigger 'lone? Some of dese days dey'll steal dat nigger—dat are a fact."

ELIZA AND LIZZIE, CHILDREN OF DRED SCOTT.

DRED SCOTT. PHOTOGRAPHED BY FITZGIBBON, OF ST. LOUIS.

HIS WIFE, HARRIET. PHOTOGRAPHED BY FITZGIBBON, OF ST. LOUIS.

◀ 1857 article about Dred Scott's life with pictures of his family

Freedom for Dred Scott

Dred Scott was a slave until after his Supreme Court case. At that point, an abolitionist purchased Scott and his wife. They were then set free. Dred Scott died nine months later.

The Dred Scott Decision

Dred Scott was a slave. His owner was an army doctor who lived in Missouri. Missouri was a slave state. Scott's owner moved to the free state of Illinois and then the free territory of Wisconsin. He took Scott with him. This meant Scott lived where slavery was against the law.

With the help of some abolitionists, Scott sued for his freedom. He thought that he should be free since he had lived in a free state and a free territory.

In 1857, the case went all the way to the United States **Supreme Court**. After a trial, the judges said that slaves were property. And, slaves had no rights under the Constitution. It was illegal for slaves to sue in court because they were not **citizens** (SIT-uh-zuhnz). Scott remained a slave.

Scott lost the court case. But, his case was very important in the years leading up to the Civil War. It made northern abolitionists very angry. This case also widened the gap between the two parts of the country.

Going Back and Forth

Dred Scott's legal case started in 1846. At first, it was ruled that he should be freed. Then, the Missouri Supreme Court reversed the ruling. So, Scott **appealed** (uh-PEELD). This means he asked the courts to study his case again. The case went to the Supreme Court. The whole process took 11 years.

John Brown's Raid

An abolitionist named John Brown believed slavery was a sin. He felt he was doing God's will by trying to end slavery. Brown gathered a small group of black and white men. His plan was to break into an **armory** (AR-muh-ree) at Harper's Ferry, Virginia. He wanted to steal guns and give them to slaves. Brown hoped to lead the slaves into a **rebellion** (ri-BEL-yuhn) against their owners.

John Brown

Speaking Out

Some people who were against slavery felt that Brown's raid was a crime. Frederick Douglass warned Brown before the raid. Douglass told Brown that his plan would fail. Douglass worried that the raid would anger the nation and be a trap for Brown.

Washington Is Captured

John Brown took some hostages during his raid. A man named Lewis Washington was one of them. He was the great-grandnephew of President George Washington. Brown stole George Washington's sword and wore it around his waist during the raid.

In October 1859, Brown broke into the Harper's Ferry armory. Shots and fighting broke out when the townspeople found out what had happened. More than 17 men were killed. Brown and his men hid in an old firehouse.

President James Buchanan ordered Colonel Robert E. Lee to stop the rebellion. Lee and his soldiers traveled to Harper's Ferry and stopped the fighting. John Brown was taken to prison. He was found guilty of **treason** (TREE-zuhn), **conspiracy** (kuhn-SPEAR-uh-see), and murder. John Brown was hanged on December 2, 1859.

▼ Soldiers forced Brown's men out of their hiding place.

The Little Giant

Stephen Douglas was called the "Little Giant." He was considered short by many at just over five feet (1.5 meters) tall. But, he had a powerful voice. Many people listened to what he had to say.

Senator Stephen Douglas was a powerful public speaker.

Lincoln-Douglas Debates

In 1858, Abraham Lincoln ran against Stephen Douglas for the Illinois Senate seat. They held many **debates** in their home state. Their debates became famous. Douglas won this election. Then, in 1860 the two men ran against each other for president. This time, Lincoln won the election.

Lincoln and Douglas had very different views on slavery. Douglas said that slavery should continue in the states where the **majority** (muh-JOR-uh-tee) of people wanted it. He did not think blacks and whites were equal. Douglas also felt that only white men should serve in the government.

Lincoln was against slavery. He felt blacks should have the same rights as whites. He said, "I believe this government cannot endure permanently half slave and half free . . . . It will become all one thing, or all the other." Lincoln did not believe the people in the United States could keep fighting like they had. He thought that the country needed to become all slave states or all free states.

Slavery in Illinois

Slavery was illegal in Illinois, the state where both Lincoln and Douglas lived. But, many people there were still **prejudiced** (PREJ-uh-dist) against blacks. Black people were not allowed to vote, go to school, or be elected to an office in Illinois.

◀ Lincoln and Douglas debated throughout Illinois.

Lincoln Is Elected

Lincoln was the Republican candidate for president in 1860. This was a new political party. This party was against slavery. But, Lincoln planned to leave slavery alone where it already existed. He said, "I have no lawful right to interfere with slavery." His goal was to stop slavery from spreading to the West.

Above all else, Lincoln wanted to keep the Union together. He quoted the Bible by saying, "A house divided against itself cannot stand." He said he would keep the Union together, even if it meant going to war.

Receiving Hate Letters

Abraham Lincoln got many angry letters during the 1860 election. Some Southerners were upset that he opposed slavery. Some Northerners sent mean letters, too. They were scared that Lincoln would destroy the Union.

Lincoln ran for president in 1860.

▲ President Lincoln taking his oath of office in 1861

Lincoln earned less than half of the votes in the election. In the South, his name was not even printed on some of the **ballots**. However, he won the majority of the **electoral** (uh-LEK-ter-uhl) **votes**. So, he became the sixteenth president of the United States.

Lincoln in Disguise

Lincoln had to wear a disguise on his trip to Washington to take office. He traveled at night because of death threats. Lincoln's wife, Mary Todd Lincoln, had many nightmares about these threats.

The Country Breaks Apart

The Southerners were angry that Abraham Lincoln was elected. They thought the government should stay out of their lives. They were still upset about the Missouri Compromise from 1820. And, they believed the Compromise of 1850 gave too much to the North. They felt these laws were threats to their rights and freedoms.

South Carolina seceded from the Union in December 1860. This was just after Lincoln was elected as president. Lincoln hoped no other states would secede. Soon, more states followed South Carolina. The Confederate States of America (or CSA) was formed by these states. Jefferson Davis became the president of this new country.

▼ Davis being inaugurated as president of the CSA

Jefferson Davis

The Confederate government took over forts, post offices, and other government locations in the South. The United States of America were no longer united. The Civil War was about to begin.

Forming a New State

West Virginia was formed after Virginia seceded from the Union. The people in West Virginia did not want to allow slavery. They joined the Union in 1863 as their own state.

▼ This map shows how the country was divided during the Civil War.

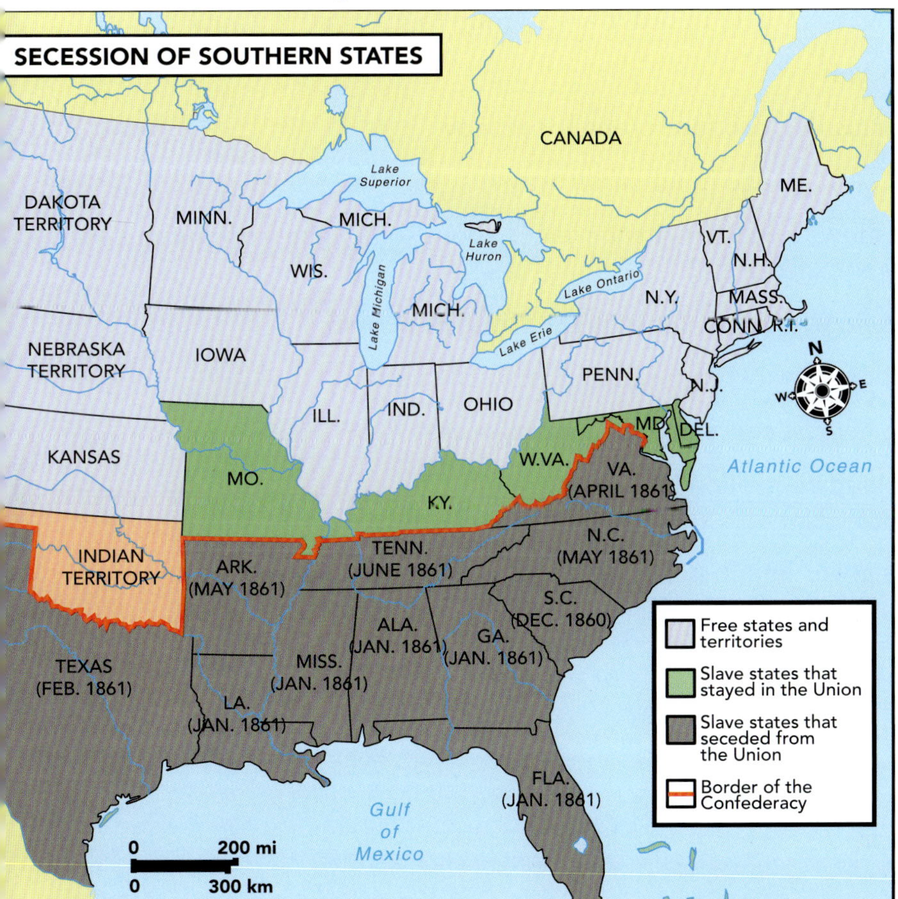

Everyone Voted Yes

South Carolina was the only state in which all of the representatives voted yes to secede. All of the other states had some representatives who voted no.

Glossary

abolitionists—people who wanted to end slavery

appealed—reviewed a court's decision at a higher level of the justice system

armory—a place where guns and weapons are stored

ballots—papers used during an election to record votes

citizens—people who are members of a country

compromising—each side giving in a bit to reach an agreement

conspiracy—a secret agreement between people to do something illegal

debates—formal talks between people about important issues

electoral votes—the votes of people who elect the president as part of the Electoral College

hostages—prisoners who are held in order for a group to get what it wants

majority—more than half

plantations—large farms that produce crops for money

prejudiced—to think of someone in an unfair way

rebellion—action to show one's thoughts or anger about something with which you disagree

representatives—people who speak for a larger group of people

secede—to leave or break away from; states leaving the Union

Supreme Court—the highest court in the United States

territories—areas of land controlled by a country, but outside the borders of the country

treason—betraying a government; not being loyal to a government or country